DINOSAURS

DINOSAURS

Consultant Editor
Dr. John Long

FOG CITY PRESS

Published by Fog City Press
814 Montgomery Street
San Francisco, CA 94133 USA

Copyright © 2005 Weldon Owen Pty Ltd
This edition printed 2007

**Chief Executive Officer,
Weldon Owen Group:** John Owen
Chief Executive Officer and President: Terry Newell
Chief Financial Officer, Weldon Owen Inc.: Simon Fraser
Vice President International Sales: Stuart Laurence
Publisher: Sheena Coupe
Creative Director: Sue Burk
Managing Editor (revised edition): Karen Penzes
Project Editor: Jennifer Losco
Series Design: Nika Markovtzev
Project Designers: Nika Markovtzev, Helen Perks
Editorial Coordinators: Irene Mickaiel, Lucie Parker
Production Director: Chris Hemesath
Sales Manager: Emily Bartle
Cover Design: Kelly Booth

ISBN-10: 1-74089-559-2
ISBN-13: 978-1-74089-559-0

Color reproduction by SC (Sang Choy) International Pte Ltd
Printed by SNP Leefung Printers Ltd
Printed in China

A Weldon Owen Production

Contents

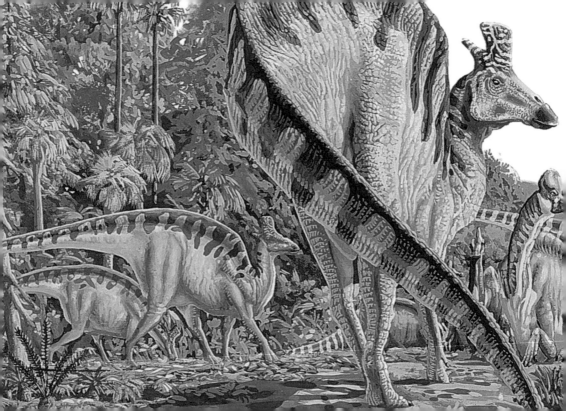

MEET THE DINOSAURS

Before the Dinosaurs

Earth began about 4,600 million years ago. Clues to the distant past can be found in ancient rocks, and the fossils they contain. Earth's long history is divided into different periods, during which a range of life forms developed and died out.

Algae

Jellyfish

Ammonite

Trilobite

WINGED INSECTS
Some ancient dragonflies had wingspans as large as 30 inches (75 cm).

Drepanaspis

Scorpion

Ornithosuchus

Hylonomus

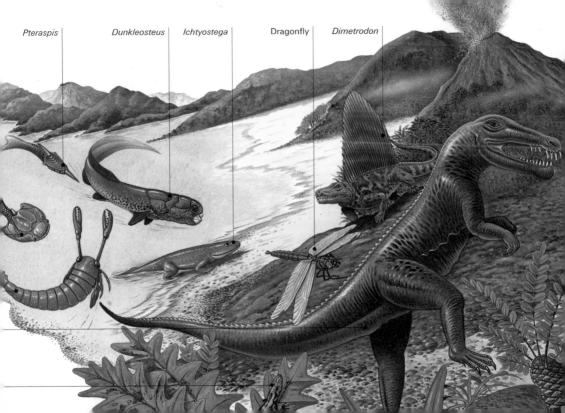

Pteraspis   *Dunkleosteus*   *Ichtyostega*   Dragonfly   *Dimetrodon*

Earth Time

From the beginning of Earth to the end of the Permian period, life evolved from single-celled algae and bacteria, through a variety of sea creatures, to early reptiles. These were the ancestors of the dinosaurs.

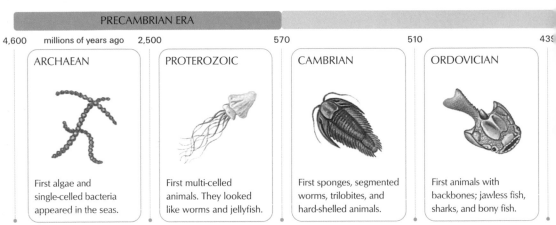

PRECAMBRIAN ERA			

4,600   millions of years ago   2,500   570   510   439

ARCHAEAN

First algae and single-celled bacteria appeared in the seas.

PROTEROZOIC

First multi-celled animals. They looked like worms and jellyfish.

CAMBRIAN

First sponges, segmented worms, trilobites, and hard-shelled animals.

ORDOVICIAN

First animals with backbones; jawless fish, sharks, and bony fish.

Trilobite fossil

Snakefly fossil

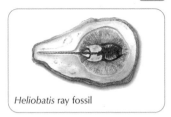

Heliobatis ray fossil

PALEOZOIC ERA

| 408 | 362 | 290 | 245 |

SILURIAN

First land plants. Sea scorpions 7 feet (2 m) dominated the seas.

DEVONIAN

The Age of Fishes and first land animals with backbones.

CARBONIFEROUS

The Age of Amphibians. Primitive reptiles hunted amphibians and insects.

PERMIAN

Many species of reptiles that ate plants and meat. Trilobites disappeared.

Dinosaur Time

Millions of years before the first human ancestors appeared, dinosaurs ruled Earth. The Age of Dinosaurs lasted 160 million years, during the Mesozoic era. This era is divided into the Triassic, Jurassic, and Cretaceous periods.

FEATURES IN COMMON

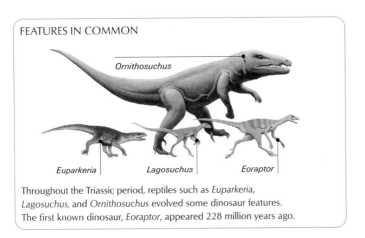

Ornithosuchus

Euparkeria   *Lagosuchus*   *Eoraptor*

Throughout the Triassic period, reptiles such as *Euparkeria*, *Lagosuchus*, and *Ornithosuchus* evolved some dinosaur features. The first known dinosaur, *Eoraptor*, appeared 228 million years ago.

245   millions of years ago   208

TRIASSIC

First dinosaurs appeared. Small meat eaters were followed by plant eaters.

Conifer pine fossil

Cycad fossil

Ginko fossil

MESOZOIC ERA		CENOZOIC ERA	

144   65   2   0

JURASSIC

The rise of the dinosaur. Dinosaurs diversified and the first birds evolved.

CRETACEOUS

Flowers bloomed. Many new dinosaurs appeared before mass extinction.

TERTIARY

The Age of Mammals. They replaced dinosaurs and dominated Earth.

QUATERNARY

The Age of Humans. They became the new rulers of Earth.

Present Day

What Is a Dinosaur?

The dinosaurs were all reptiles and laid hard-shelled eggs like those of snakes. Some had the same dry, scaly skin that lizards and crocodiles have today. Some also had feathers. When you think about dinosaurs, you may imagine huge, ferocious creatures—still frightening even though they are extinct. But not all dinosaurs were large. Not all were scary. In fact, an amazing thing about these animals is how different they were from one another.

JURASSIC HUNTERS
69-foot (21-m) *Apatosaurus* munches on a cycad while 7-foot (2-m) *Ornitholestes* pounces on a salamander disturbed by the grazing giant.

Plant-eating dinosaur species 65%   Meat eaters 35%

PLANT EATERS
AND MEAT EATERS
Many more dinosaurs ate plants than ate meat. If we could count the individual dinosaurs that lived, the proportion of plant eaters would be even greater.

Dinosaur Diversity

Today we know about more than 800 different types of dinosaurs. Paleontologists think we will eventually discover more than 1,000. But there are many dinosaurs that we will never know anything about—they are the dinosaurs that left no fossils behind to tell us about themselves.

Parasaurolophus
Late Cretaceous

Ouranosaurus
Early Cretaceous

Tyrannosaurus
Late Cretaceous

Triceratops
Late Cretaceous

Struthiomimus
Late Cretaceous

Maiasaura
Late Cretaceous

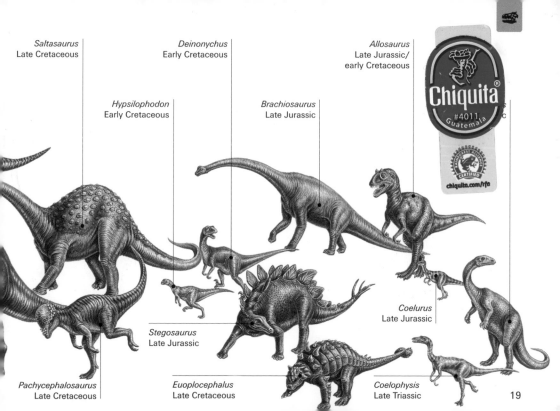

Saltasaurus
Late Cretaceous

Deinonychus
Early Cretaceous

Allosaurus
Late Jurassic/
early Cretaceous

Hypsilophodon
Early Cretaceous

Brachiosaurus
Late Jurassic

Stegosaurus
Late Jurassic

Coelurus
Late Jurassic

Pachycephalosaurus
Late Cretaceous

Euoplocephalus
Late Cretaceous

Coelophysis
Late Triassic

19

Look-alikes

Look carefully at these animals. Do you think they are dinosaurs? Some of them are certainly prehistoric, and they may resemble dinosaurs physically, but in fact none of them is a dinosaur. Dinosaurs ruled the land, but marine reptiles dominated the sea, and flying reptiles, called pterosaurs, glided through the skies.

FOSSIL SKELETONS
Fossil skeletons of pliosaurs have been discovered in most parts of the world. This marine creature grew 16 feet (5 m) long.

DIMETRODON

Synapsids, mammal-like reptiles, lived before the dinosaurs.

PELEONEUSTES

Dinosaurs did not live in the sea. That was the home of marine reptiles.

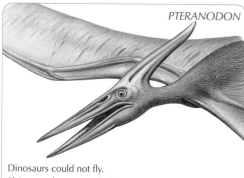

PTERANODON

Dinosaurs could not fly.
Flying reptiles were called pterosaurs.

KOMODO DRAGON

Do not let this Komodo dragon
fool you. It is the world's largest living lizard.

Famous Finds

In 1822, Mary Mantell found some fossil teeth in a quarry. Her husband, Gideon Mantell, thought the teeth belonged to a giant plant-eating animal and began digging for more clues. When he realized the teeth were from an extinct reptile, he named the creature *Iguanodon* because he thought it looked like a giant iguana.

DOWN IN THE SWAMP
In 1878, almost 40 *Iguanodon* skeletons were found in Belgium. This was the first opportunity to study many complete dinosaurs.

THE MYSTERY TEETH
Gideon realized that, though larger, the teeth were similar to an iguana's.

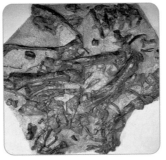

THE SLAB OF BONES
In 1834, some of Gideon's friends bought him these *Iguanodon* bones.

THE FIRST *IGUANODON*
After studying the bones, Gideon drew this picture of *Iguanodon*.

Amazing Discoveries

New fossil discoveries gave better clues to *Iguanodon*. Richard Owen, an animal expert, realized the fossils came from a new group of animals, which he called dinosaurs. Owen's ideas led to "dinosaur-mania," and soon dinosaur detectives were busy unearthing these ancient reptiles.

WILD WEST DINOSAUR RACE
Othniel Marsh (top, center) and his team discovered hundreds of new dinosaur species during the great dinosaur-bone race of the late 1800s.

IGUANODON, 1853

This sculpture shows a heavy animal with a rhinoceros horn.

THUMB SPIKE

After much study, scientists realized the "horn" was a thumb spike.

FOSSIL TRACKS

Iguanodon fossil tracks have been found all over the world.

25

Naming Dinosaurs

"Dinosaur" means "a fearfully great, or terrible, lizard." The English paleontologist Richard Owen invented the word in 1841. He is called the father of the dinosaurs and has described hundreds of ancient animals.

Some dinosaurs were named after the place where their fossils were first found. Others were named after a particular habit we believe they had, or an unusual physical feature that was special to them.

EDMONTONIA

Edmontonia means "of Edmonton," which is the Canadian province where it was discovered.

OVIRAPTOR

Oviraptor was named "egg thief" because it was discovered lying over a nest of dinosaur eggs.

TYRANNOSAURUS

Tyrannosaurus was built for attack. Its name means "tyrant lizard."

TRICERATOPS

Triceratops means "three-horned face." It was named for this distinctive feature.

27

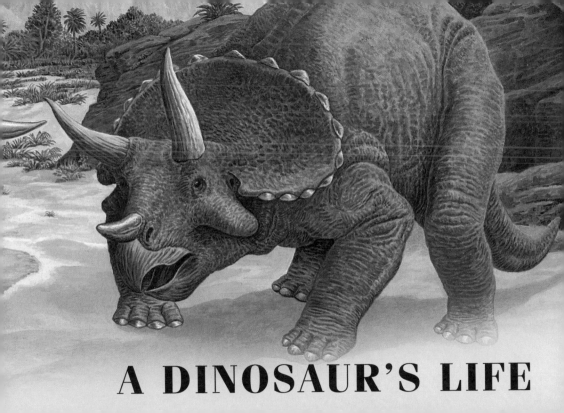

A DINOSAUR'S LIFE

Meat Eaters

Meat-eating dinosaurs were lean, mean, killing machines. Their bodies were designed to capture, kill, and tear apart prey. They gave chase on two strong legs, and some grabbed their prey with their hands. For the final kill, they chomped down with their mouthful of murderously sharp teeth, which were serrated like steak knives. The meat-eating dinosaurs are all from one group, known as theropods.

KILLER KICK
Deinonychus kicks out at its next victim. It had sharp teeth and claws on its hands and feet.

HEAD-ON
Tyrannosaurus had a
huge mouth with more
than 50 stabbing teeth.

Plant Eaters

There were hundreds, probably even thousands, of different plant-eating dinosaurs. It is not easy to survive just on plants because they are not as nutritious as meat. But in the warm, wet Mesozoic era, plants grew so thickly that dinosaurs had plenty to choose from. Their diet depended on what plants they could reach and what their mouths, teeth, and stomachs could handle. Here, two *Stegosaurus* feed on low-growing ferns. Their front legs were shorter than their back legs, making it easier to keep their heads down near food.

Long-necks

The biggest, heaviest, and longest land animals that have ever lived on Earth were the sauropod dinosaurs. All the sauropods had incredibly long necks with tiny heads on top. These dinosaurs had appetites as huge as their bodies, and spent most of the day munching through the tons of food they needed to keep their stomachs full.

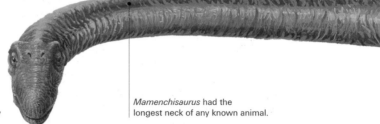

Mamenchisaurus had the longest neck of any known animal.

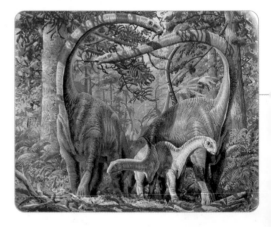

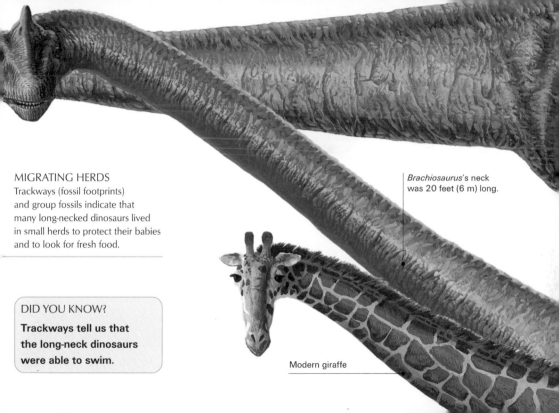

MIGRATING HERDS
Trackways (fossil footprints)
and group fossils indicate that
many long-necked dinosaurs lived
in small herds to protect their babies
and to look for fresh food.

Brachiosaurus's neck
was 20 feet (6 m) long.

DID YOU KNOW?
**Trackways tell us that
the long-neck dinosaurs
were able to swim.**

Modern giraffe

Head Cases

Dinosaurs were wearing some strange headgear toward the end of the Cretaceous period. Some had crests, spikes, prongs, and sacs. They were the hadrosaurs, or duckbilled dinosaurs, named for their broad, ducklike beaks. The pachycephalosaurs, or boneheaded dinosaurs, had thick domes of solid bone on their skulls that they used as crash helmets. Both these dinosaur goups ate many types of plants.

HEAD TO HEAD
Two male *Pachycephalosaurus* butt heads like mountain goats to see which will mate with the females. One of them has become dizzy and is about to plummet to its death.

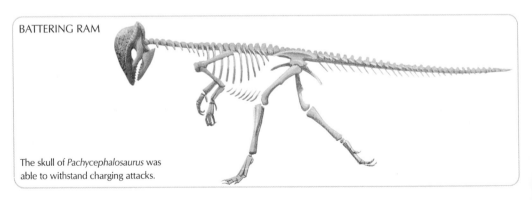

BATTERING RAM

The skull of *Pachycephalosaurus* was able to withstand charging attacks.

Armor, Plates, and Horns

Some plant-eating dinosaurs were built to stand and fight off an attacker. They were armed with spikes and horns, and protected by plates and shields. This array of weaponry helped them defend themselves, but the armor was heavy and prevented a quick getaway. An angry *Triceratops* (right) on the attack would have been an awesome sight.

Side by Side

It was a daily fight for survival in the dinosaur world. Plant eaters and meat eaters had to fight to find enough to eat while making sure they did not get eaten themselves. Some dinosaurs were larger than a bus and romped along on four legs. Others were no bigger than a chicken and cruised about on two legs.

The Dinosaur Walk

Dinosaurs sometimes walked upright with their legs beneath their bodies. They are the only reptiles that have ever been able to do this. As they did not have to move from side to side to walk, they could breathe easily while running quickly.

SPRAWLING

Lizards sprawl when they walk. They must twist their whole body and lift each leg one at a time.

HALFWAY UP

Some reptiles have upright hind legs. They can run on their hind legs for short distances.

ON TWO LEGS

A dinosaur's weight was supported by its straight legs, tucked under its body. This made them fast movers.

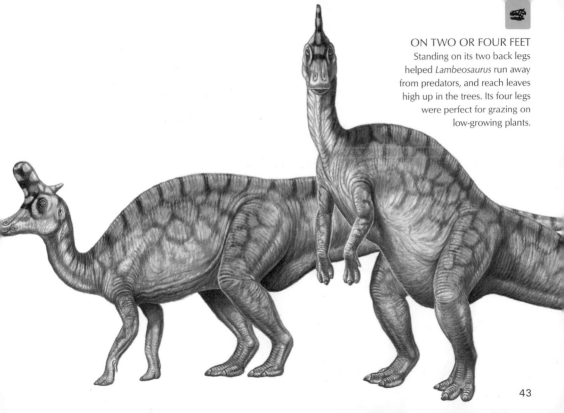

Standing on its two back legs
helped *Lambeosaurus* run away
from predators, and reach leaves
high up in the trees. Its four legs
were perfect for grazing on
low-growing plants.

Dinosaur Hips

Dinosaurs can be divided into two groups, depending on what type of hips they had. The saurischian group had hips that looked like a lizard's, so they are called the lizard-hipped dinosaurs. Ornithischians had birdlike hips. They are the bird-hipped dinosaurs.

Ilium

Ischium

Pubis

FAST-MOVING MEAT EATER
Allosaurus was a saurischian. Its pubis pointed forward between the legs and helped support the leg muscles for fast running and hunting.

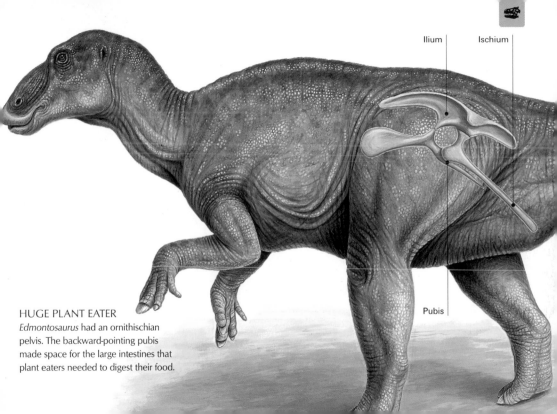

Ilium

Ischium

Pubis

HUGE PLANT EATER

Edmontosaurus had an ornithischian
pelvis. The backward-pointing pubis
made space for the large intestines that
plant eaters needed to digest their food.

Warm-blooded or Cold-blooded?

If animals get too hot or too cold their bodies cannot work properly. They regulate their body temperature in two different ways. Cold-blooded animals, such as snakes, get their body heat from outside. They sunbathe until they warm up, then they move into the shade. Warm-blooded animals, such as humans, generate heat inside their bodies by converting energy from the food they eat. Scientists believe that some dinosaurs were cold-blooded while others were warm-blooded.

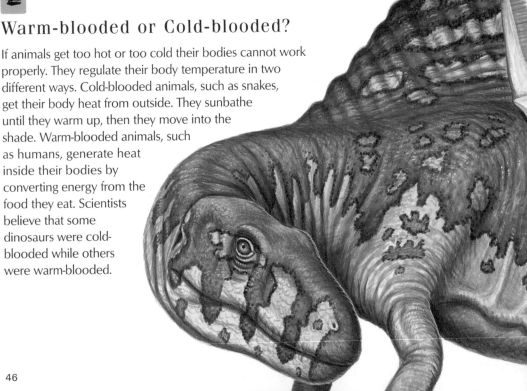

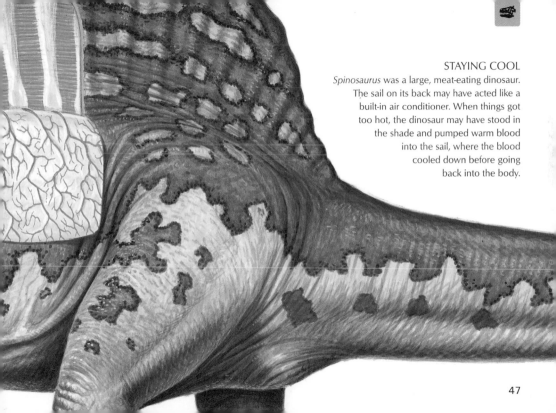

STAYING COOL

Spinosaurus was a large, meat-eating dinosaur. The sail on its back may have acted like a built-in air conditioner. When things got too hot, the dinosaur may have stood in the shade and pumped warm blood into the sail, where the blood cooled down before going back into the body.

Keeping Warm; Staying Cool

LONG NECK, TAIL, AND LEGS

A long neck, long tail, and long legs all helped *Diplodocus* get rid of excess heat so it did not go into meltdown.

HOT PLATES

Tuojiangosaurus

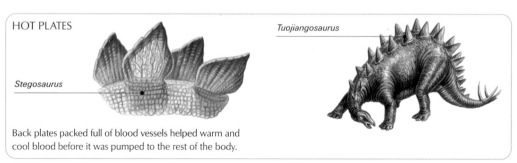

Stegosaurus

Back plates packed full of blood vessels helped warm and cool blood before it was pumped to the rest of the body.

DINOSAUR IN THE DARK

Winter days in Australia were dark and cold during the Cretaceous period. *Leaellynasaura* may have been warm-blooded to survive in a place where the Sun did not shine.

LETTING OFF STEAM

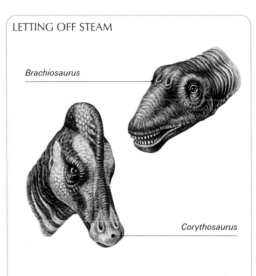

Brachiosaurus

Corythosaurus

Some dinosaurs could let off steam by pumping blood through the delicate skin inside their huge nostrils. This helped them stay cool.

Dinosaur Diets

There was plenty of dinosaur food in the Jurassic world. Meat eaters that did not eat other dinosaurs gobbled up turtles, crocodiles, lizards, and insects. Plant eaters liked to nibble on the leaves from ferns and trees. They had many plants to choose from.

DINOSAUR HABITAT
The earliest dinosaurs ate meat, while later plant-eating dinosaurs enjoyed the lush plant life around them.

Plesiochelys, a turtle

Dragonfly

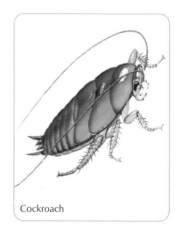

Cockroach

Horsetail

Ginkgo

Cycad

Teeth, Mouths, and Beaks

You can tell a lot about a plant eater and what it ate by the type of teeth it had and the shape of its mouth or beak. Giraffes' teeth are different from zebras' teeth because giraffes eat tender leaves from the tops of trees, while zebras eat tough, dry grass. In the same way, different families of dinosaurs had different kinds of teeth and beaks to cope with the different types of plants they ate.

SNIP AND SWALLOW

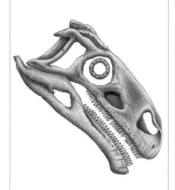

Plateosaurus had small, weak teeth that worked like scissors, snipping off mouthfuls of soft leaves. *Plateosaurus* could not chew. It swallowed food whole.

PLUCK AND GRIND

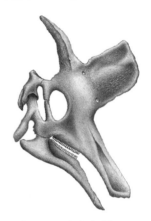

Lambeosaurus plucked off leaves and fruit with its horny beak, ground them up, and then swallowed. Grinding wore its teeth down, but it had hundreds of replacements.

NIP AND GRIND

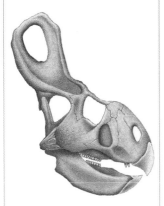

Protoceratops had a parrot-like beak at the front of its mouth for nipping off leaves. Teeth at the back of its mouth then ground them into a paste.

CUT, STAB, AND CHOP

Heterodontosaurus had three kinds of teeth. It had small cutting teeth at the front of its mouth. Then it had two sets of stabbing, fanglike teeth, and chopping teeth in the back.

STRIP AND SWALLOW

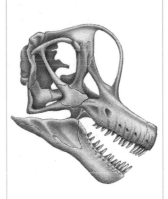

Brachiosaurus had teeth that looked like chisels. It stripped the leaves from tall trees with these teeth but could not chew its food up before swallowing.

Dinner Tools

QUICK HANDS

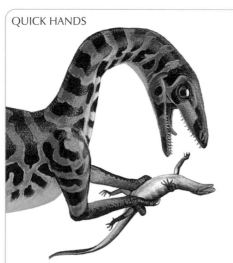

Compsognathus was a very small dinosaur that used its hands to catch and eat its lizard dinners. Its cutting teeth sliced easily through flesh, and large chunks were swallowed whole.

BIG MOUTH

Tyrannosaurus had teeth like stabbing pegs. They were up to 6 inches (15 cm) long! The teeth could not cut or chew, but with their razor-sharp serrations they could pierce and tear huge chunks of meat.

NO TEETH

Some meat eaters did not have teeth. Instead, they had sharp, narrow beaks, perfect for catching the food they liked. *Gallimimus* probably snapped up insects and small animals, or swallowed eggs in one gulp.

FISHING HOOK

Scientists have found fish scales in the stomach of *Baryonyx*. It probably speared slippery fish with the huge hook on its hand. Then it held the fish in its long jaw before swallowing.

On the Hunt

Meat eaters needed good eyes, and a plan of attack, to hunt prey that was armored or much larger than themselves. They probably hunted in packs, jumping on larger animals or terrorizing smaller ones.

GROUP ATTACK
A *Barosaurus* mother rears up to protect her baby from an *Allosaurus* attack.

FIGHTING FOR LIFE
Tenontosaurus, a plant eater
from the early Cretaceous
period, fights a pack of
ferocious *Deinonychus.*
This reconstructed scene
may well have happened.
In the USA, the fossil
skeleton of a *Tenontosaurus*
was found surrounded by
five scattered specimens
of *Deinonychus.*

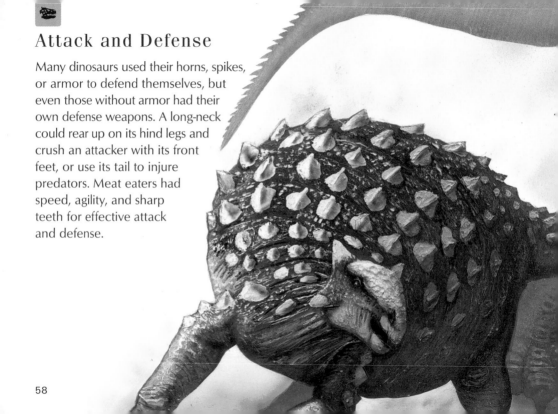

Attack and Defense

Many dinosaurs used their horns, spikes, or armor to defend themselves, but even those without armor had their own defense weapons. A long-neck could rear up on its hind legs and crush an attacker with its front feet, or use its tail to injure predators. Meat eaters had speed, agility, and sharp teeth for effective attack and defense.

ON THE ATTACK

The *Ankylosaurus* stands its ground and takes a swipe at an attacking *Tyrannosaurus* with its tail. One direct hit to the ankles by the huge bony club on the end could cripple the *Tyrannosaurus*. Sharp studs and slabs of bone protect the back of *Ankylosaurus*, but one bite to its soft underbelly from the powerful jaws of *Tyrannosaurus* would finish it off.

The Armored Division

SPIKE

Tuojiangosaurus had a serious set of tail spikes. With one swing of its tail, this plant eater could puncture a predator's belly.

CLUB

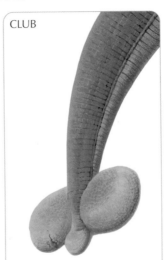

Euoplocephalus injured predators by lashing out with the bony club at the end of its tail. It was hard for them to get close enough to attack.

WHIP

Diplodocus could lash out at attackers with stinging blows. Its tail was almost as long as a tennis court, and worked like a whip.

PREDATORS BEWARE!

Styracosaurus defends its young from a predator by displaying its nose horn and spiked head shield. Its spiky frill protected its neck, and it could use its nose horn to rip open a predator.

DID YOU KNOW?

The neck of *Triceratops* was protected by a sheet of solid bone like a shield.

Camouflage

We do not know what colors dinosaurs were, but we know what environments they lived in. The right colors help hide an animal in its surroundings, camouflaged from both predators and unwary prey.

STRIPES

Coelophysis was a swift predator like a tiger. Perhaps *Coelophysis* also had stripes like a tiger. Stripes help camouflage an animal's shape so its prey does not see it coming before it strikes.

SPOTS

Dryosaurus was a small plant eater that lived in forests, as many deer do today. Deer have light spots on a darker background, similar to the dappled light in forests.

PLAIN COLORS

Edmontosaurus lived in herds and migrated across continents like today's antelopes. Neutral colors may have helped *Edmontosaurus* blend in on the open plains.

Speed

Sleek and speedy dinosaurs zipped through the Mesozoic landscape. Some were plant eaters, in a hurry to get away from hungry predators, but small meat eaters, with their streamlined bodies and long back legs, were the really fast movers of the dinosaur world.

We can tell how fast a dinosaur ran by looking at its fossilized footprints and its body shape and structure. Although the fastest dinosaurs would have easily outpaced a running human, they would have been no match for an ostrich, let alone a cheetah.

Fastest human
22.8 mph (36.5 km/h)

Dromiceiomimus
37 mph (60 km/h)

Ostrich
45 mph (72 km/h)

Cheetah
60 mph (100 km/h)

CAN'T CATCH
GALLIMIMUS
When *Gallimimus* got going
there was no way *Albertosaurus*
could catch it. *Gallimimus* could
run at 30 miles (48 km) per hour.

Brain Power

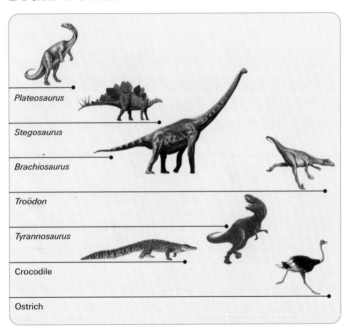

Plateosaurus

Stegosaurus

Brachiosaurus

Troödon

Tyrannosaurus

Crocodile

Ostrich

The intelligence of dinosaurs is estimated by comparing the size of their brain to their body size. The "thinking" part of a dinosaur's brain, the cerebrum, was much smaller than a mammal's. This meant that a dinosaur could not have learnt new things as easily as a dog or monkey could today.

BIG AND SMALL

The smartest dinosaurs were small, fast-moving meat eaters from the late Cretaceous period. They were as smart as an ostrich, and much smarter than a crocodile. Plant eaters could survive with smaller brains.

SMALL BRAIN

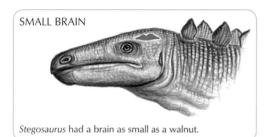

Stegosaurus had a brain as small as a walnut.

BIG BRAIN

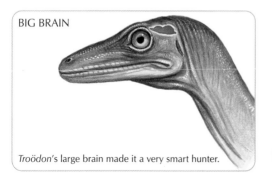

Troödon's large brain made it a very smart hunter.

BRAIN SIZE COMPARISON

Tyrannosaurus had one of the biggest dinosaur heads, but a very small brain. A human head, on the other hand, is mostly brain, to be able to think and also run the body.

Senses

It's not easy to find out from a pile of fossils what dinosaurs could see. But certain dinosaur skeletons give scientists some clues. Touch is the toughest sense for scientists to understand about an extinct animal. With its thick, scaly skin, a dinosaur's sense of touch must have been very different from ours.

TOUCH

This fossil shows an impression of *Polacanthus* skin. Some dinosaurs may also have been covered in feathers.

TASTE AND SMELL

Iguanodon had a good sense of taste and smell, so it might have sniffed out hidden predators or distant plants.

SIGHT

Troödon probably had a good sense of sight, and may have been able to see in the dark.

HEARING

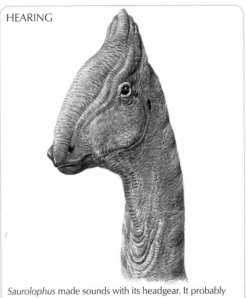

Saurolophus made sounds with its headgear. It probably had good hearing to listen out for the herd's replies.

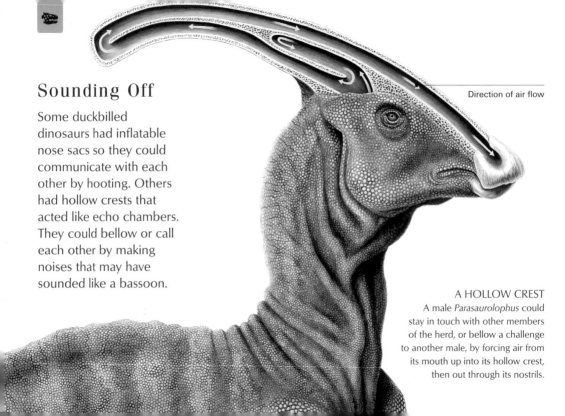

Sounding Off

Some duckbilled dinosaurs had inflatable nose sacs so they could communicate with each other by hooting. Others had hollow crests that acted like echo chambers. They could bellow or call each other by making noises that may have sounded like a bassoon.

Direction of air flow

A HOLLOW CREST
A male *Parasaurolophus* could stay in touch with other members of the herd, or bellow a challenge to another male, by forcing air from its mouth up into its hollow crest, then out through its nostrils.

SPIKE AND SAC

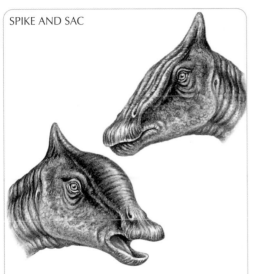

Saurolophus had a head spike and possibly also an inflatable nose sac. By blowing air into this sac, it may have called to other dinosaurs.

SOUND SAC

Edmontosaurus was a flat-headed hadrosaur with no fancy headgear. But it may have inflated a sac of skin on the front of its face to make sounds.

Weighing Them Up

One of the most amazing things about
dinosaurs is that they came in such extreme
sizes. The big and the small lived side by side.

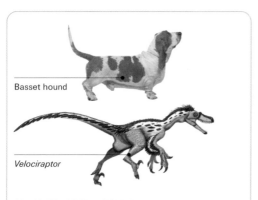

Basset hound

Velociraptor

AN AVERAGE DINOSAUR
Dinosaurs are known for their incredible size,
but most were relatively small like *Velociraptor*,
a dinosaur that grew to the size of a basset hound.

WEIGHT COMPARISONS

1 African elephant = 15 *Protoceratops*

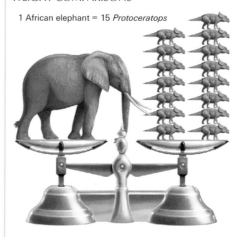

The heaviest land animal alive today
is the African elephant. It far outweighs
smaller dinosaurs such as *Protoceratops*.

1 *Tyrannosaurus* = 1 African elephant

1 *Argentinosaurus* = 17 African elephants

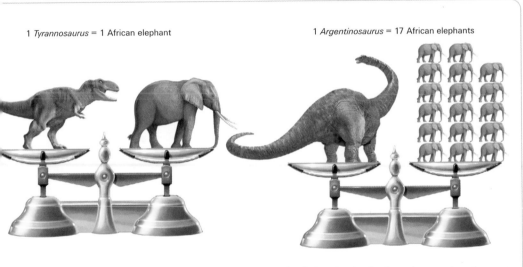

An African elephant would have matched *Tyrannosaurus* in weight. Both of them weigh 6.5 tons (6 tonnes). *Tyrannosaurus* grew taller than a double-decker bus.

An elephant is only a fraction as heavy as *Argentinosaurus* and other giant plant eaters. It takes 17 African elephants to match an 110 ton (100 tonne) *Argentinosaurus*.

Big and Small

The largest meat-eating dinosaur was *Giganotosaurus*, but even it was dwarfed by the plant-eating sauropods, or long-necks. The longest dinosaur that ever lived was probably *Seismosaurus*. The smallest plant eater, at just 20 inches (50 cm) long, was *Icropachycephalosaurus*.

Smallest meat eater:
Microraptor
31 inches (80 cm) long
and 10 inches (25 cm) tall

Longest dinosaur: *Seismosaurus*
150 feet (45 m) long and
18 feet (5.5 m) high at shoulder

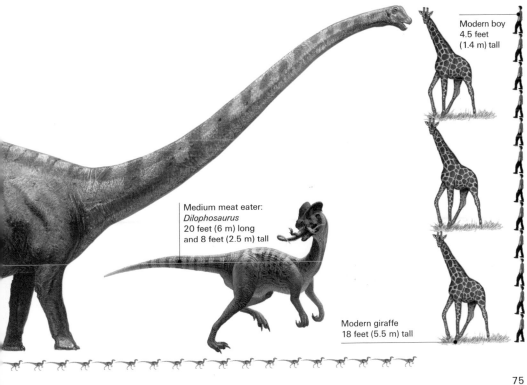

Modern boy
4.5 feet
(1.4 m) tall

Medium meat eater:
Dilophosaurus
20 feet (6 m) long
and 8 feet (2.5 m) tall

Modern giraffe
18 feet (5.5 m) tall

Skeleton of a Giant

This skeleton belongs to *Barosaurus*, a sauropod that grew to 89 feet (27 m) long. Scientists once thought that sauropods were too heavy to walk on land. Now we know that their skeletons had hollow spaces, which helped them to weigh less yet still be strong.

Strong, broad hips held the weight of the body.

The legs were as straight and strong as columns.

A long, whiplike tail balanced the long neck like a seesaw.

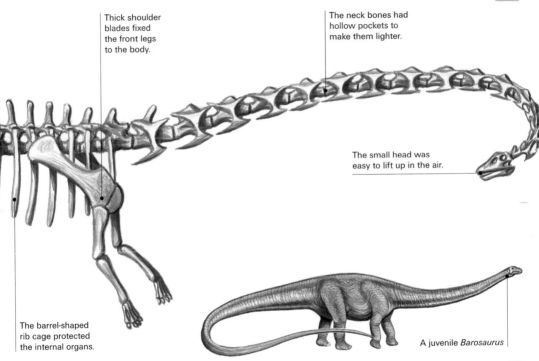

Thick shoulder blades fixed the front legs to the body.

The neck bones had hollow pockets to make them lighter.

The small head was easy to lift up in the air.

The barrel-shaped rib cage protected the internal organs.

A juvenile *Barosaurus*

Skeletons and Skulls

OURANOSAURUS

Ouranosaurus had small jaw muscles for breaking up leaves and plants.

CERATOSAURUS

A *Ceratosaurus* skull had space for huge jaw muscles.

Dinosaur skeletons came in a variety of forms. Enormous frames supported the long-necks while the smallest dinosaurs had elegant skeletons. All dinosaurs had holes in their skulls. Meat eaters had the largest holes for their powerful jaw muscles.

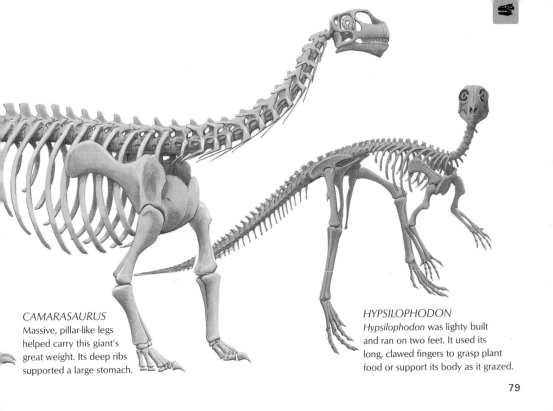

CAMARASAURUS
Massive, pillar-like legs
helped carry this giant's
great weight. Its deep ribs
supported a large stomach.

HYPSILOPHODON
Hypsilophodon was lighty built
and ran on two feet. It used its
long, clawed fingers to grasp plant
food or support its body as it grazed.

Loners and Herds

Plant eaters travelled in packs and herds to defend themselves against predators. Armored dinosaurs probably lived alone because they did not need to travel in groups for protection.

LIVING TOGETHER
Flat-headed and crested duckbills could live in herds together without taking one another's food supply.

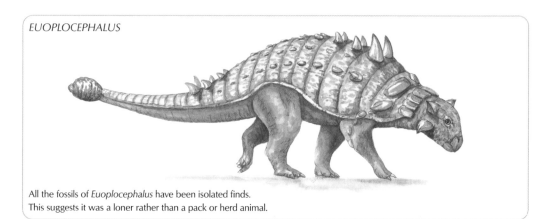

EUOPLOCEPHALUS

All the fossils of *Euoplocephalus* have been isolated finds.
This suggests it was a loner rather than a pack or herd animal.

The Next Generation

Paleontologists first thought that dinosaurs did not look after their eggs or their young because very few dinosaur nests had been discovered. Then, in 1978, John Horner found a duckbill dinosaur nesting site in North America. Dozens of nests were spaced so that adult dinosaurs could guard their own eggs without stepping on another dinosaur's nest.

INSIDE AN EGG

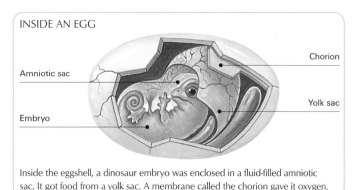

Chorion

Amniotic sac

Yolk sac

Embryo

Inside the eggshell, a dinosaur embryo was enclosed in a fluid-filled amniotic sac. It got food from a yolk sac. A membrane called the chorion gave it oxygen.

FEEDING TIME
A mother *Oviraptor* returns to her nest of hungry babies. She has scavenged the carcass of a baby *Velociraptor* for their dinner.

Raising a *Maiasaura* Family

ON GUARD
John Horner named this dinosaur *Maiasaura*, or "good mother lizard," because it protected its nest.

A DINOSAUR NURSERY
Up to 25 eggs were laid in each *Maiasaura* nest. Baby hatchlings were about 18 inches (50 cm) long.

Maiasaura hatchling

One-year-old *Maiasaura*

Adult *Maiasaura*

THE AGE OF DINOSAURS

Triassic Times

The first dinosaurs appeared in the Triassic period, about 228 million years ago. They lived in an environment that would be unrecognizable to us today. It was a world with dry, red landscapes and forests without a single flower. At this time, Earth was a huge supercontinent called Pangaea.

AGILE HUNTERS
In the warm, moist forest close to the coast of Pangaea, two *Coelophysis* chase a *Planocephalosaurus* up a tree.

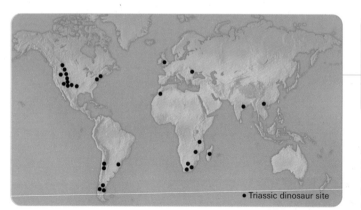

• Triassic dinosaur site

A VIEW OF THE NEW WORLD
Fossil sites show that most dinosaurs lived near the center of Pangaea, the area now divided among North America, Africa, and northern Europe.

The Arrival of Dinosaurs

The first dinosaurs were small meat eaters. Their two back legs let them stand upright and run much faster than the animals they hunted. These speedy killers soon ruled the Triassic world. Later, the first plant-eating dinosaurs started appearing.

Plateosaurus was a 26-foot (8-m) long plant eater.

Herrerasaurus was a 6½-foot (2-m) long meat eater.

Saltopus was a 2-foot (60-cm) long meat eater.

Zanclodon was a 20-foot (6-m) long meat eater.

Procompsognathus was a 4-foot (1.2-m) long meat eater.

THE TRIASSIC LANDSCAPE

Although the landscape was mainly arid, plants such as conifers, gingkoes, ferns, and cycads grew near water.

Jurassic World

During the Jurassic, Pangaea broke in two, forming
Laurasia and Gondwana. Cooler temperatures and
higher rainfall created a warm, wet climate, just right
for dinosaurs. There was good food for the plant
eaters and good stalking ground for the meat eaters.
Many new types of dinosaurs appeared in this time.

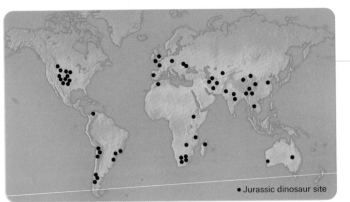

• Jurassic dinosaur site

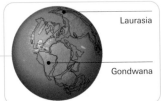

Laurasia

Gondwana

MOVING APART
The Jurassic period started
208 million years ago. Fossil sites show
that dinosaurs from the two continents
were similar but not the same.

REARING ITS HEAD
A *Diplodocus* rears to defend itself against a predator. Its clawed front feet and lashing tail are ready for battle.

A Parade of Dinosaurs

Giant long-necks ate from the tallest
trees and armored stegosaurs lumbered
on all fours. Huge and fearsome meat eaters
hunted the giant long-necks, while small meat
eaters scurried after insects and small reptiles.

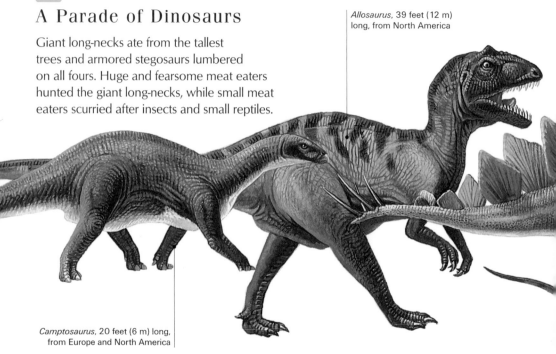

Allosaurus, 39 feet (12 m)
long, from North America

Camptosaurus, 20 feet (6 m) long,
from Europe and North America

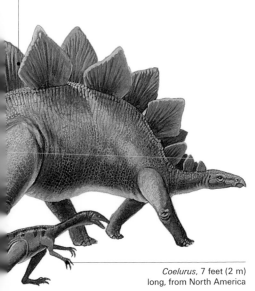

Stegosaurus, 29 feet (8.8 m) long, from North America

Coelurus, 7 feet (2 m) long, from North America

THE JURASSIC LANDSCAPE

Triassic plants diversified and huge Jurassic forests grew in the warmer, more humid climate.

Cretaceous Period

In the Cretaceous period, Laurasia and Gondwana kept moving apart and Gondwana broke up into smaller continents. The weather became more seasonal and the first flowering plants appeared. There were more types of dinosaurs than ever before. At the end of the Cretaceous, a mass extinction occurred and the dinosaurs disappeared.

PREDATORS AND PREY
A *Velociraptor* battles a *Protoceratops*, squashing dinosaur eggs in the process. *Prenocephale* watches the fierce battle.

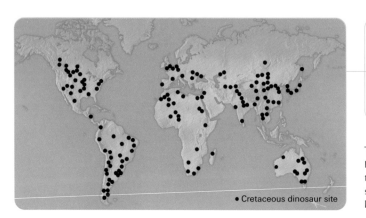

• Cretaceous dinosaur site

THE BIG BREAKUP
Finds of Cretaceous dinosaurs are the most common dinosaur fossil sites today. The Cretaceous period lasted for 80 million years.

THE CRETACEOUS LANDSCAPE

By the late Cretaceous period, oaks, magnolias, and hickories covered parts of the Northern Hemisphere.

Tyrannosaurus

Euoplocephalus

The Last of the Dinosaurs

Dinosaurs went through many changes during the Cretaceous. Some stegosaurs died out, but armored ankylosaurs took their place. The huge long-necks became less common and new plant eaters, such as the duckbills, thrived. With so much food to feast on, meat eaters like *Tyrannosaurus* appeared.

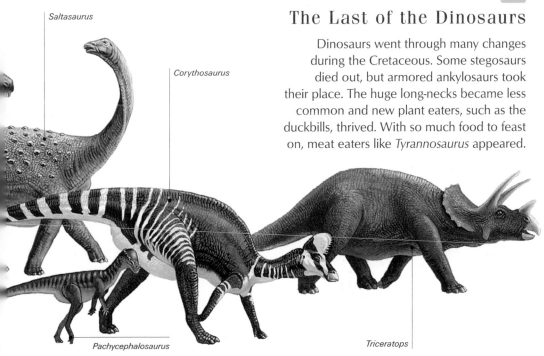

Saltasaurus

Corythosaurus

Pachycephalosaurus

Triceratops

Airborne Animals

Before birds there were the pterosaurs, the flying
reptiles of the Mesozoic era. Their fine bones
kept their bodies light enough to fly. They glided
or flapped about on wings of skin, their large eyes
on the lookout for fish and small animals to eat.

Archaeopteryx

Dimorphodon

Bee

Moth

TINY MOTHS AND SMALL, SOCIAL BEES

While many groups of insects had already evolved, moths and bees were two groups that first appeared with the dinosaurs.

Pterodaustro

Rhamphorhynchus

Marine Animals

Different types of marine reptiles competed to feed on fish, small sea creatures, and each other. The dolphin-like ichthyosaurs were fast predators, torpedoing through the water. *Liopleurodon* grew to more than 66 feet (20 m) long! That's more than three times the size of a great white shark.

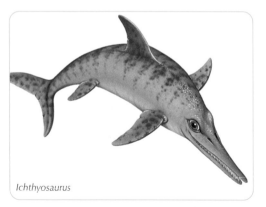

Ichthyosaurus

Liopleurodon

Elasmosaurus

Kronosaurus

Land Animals

Many groups of animals, including some that are still alive today, existed alongside the dinosaurs. They were a great food source for small, meat-eating dinosaurs. They included lizards and the first snakes, ancient mammals, and ancient crocodiles, such as *Bernissartia*, that were cousins of the dinosaurs.

Polyglyphanodon

Crusafontia

ANCIENT JAWS

Dimetrodon was an ancient mammal-like reptile that lived before the dinosaurs. Its jaws and teeth were similar to those of a modern crocodile.

Alphadon

Bernissartia

The End of an Era

After ruling Earth for 160 million years, the
dinosaurs suddenly vanished 65 million years
ago. The main theory for this mass extinction
is that a huge meteorite collided with Earth,
causing environmental chaos around the world.

METEORITE STRIKE
If a massive meteorite crashed into Earth, fire would burn
everything for thousands of miles and acid would rain down.

Other Extinction Theories

What caused the mass extinction at the end of the Cretaceous is still a mystery. It had to be powerful enough to kill 75 percent of all animals and plants, but still leave some things alive. Some scientists believe major changes in the weather, such as global warming or cooling, or a volcanic disaster help to explain why the dinosaurs disappeared.

Cool climate change

Warm climate change

Volcanic eruptions

Victims and Survivors

Pterosaurs died out, but birds did not. Dinosaurs vanished, but small land reptiles and mammals survived. In the oceans, some fish survived, but all the marine reptiles died except the turtles. Almost half the plants that thrived during the Cretaceous were no longer growing in the Tertiary period.

DEATH VALLEY, CALIFORNIA
The Tertiary world would have looked similar to this American landscape.

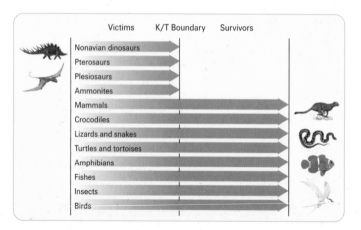

Victims	K/T Boundary	Survivors
Nonavian dinosaurs		
Pterosaurs		
Plesiosaurs		
Ammonites		
Mammals		
Crocodiles		
Lizards and snakes		
Turtles and tortoises		
Amphibians		
Fishes		
Insects		
Birds		

CRETACEOUS/ TERTIARY BOUNDARY
We still do not know for certain why some animals disappeared and others survived.

Today's Dinosaurs

The dinosaurs are dead, but it seems that certain dinosaur features live on in other animals. Dinosaurs and birds, for example, are very different animals but they have many things in common. Scientists are now convinced that dinosaurs were the ancestors of birds. The dinosaurs are also related to crocodiles, which survived the great extinction.

Dinosaur ancestor
Reptilian theropod

Feathered dinosaur
Archaeopteryx

Waterfowl ancestor
Ichthyornis

Modern waterfowl
Snow goose

113

DINOSAUR CLUES

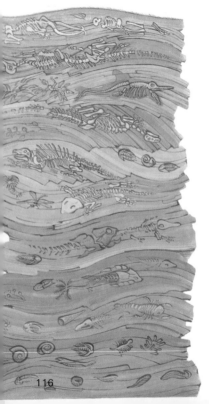

Fossil Evidence

Fossils are records of life through the ages, written in stone or rock. Anything that was once alive can leave fossil traces. Usually, only the hard parts of a plant or animal end up as fossils. By dating the layers of rocks that are found at different levels, scientists can work out the age of fossils found in them.

FROM ANIMAL TO FOSSIL
This modern, bright sea star has the same five-point form as Jurassic sea star fossils (far right) from so long ago.

Studying Fossils

Paleontologists are scientists who learn about ancient life forms by studying fossils. These can be footprints, bones, eggs, impressions, or other remains of prehistoric plants or animals. Paleontologists use fossil clues to piece together pictures of creatures that lived many millions of years ago. Many paleontologists are dinosaur experts.

DINOSAUR DETECTIVE
Varuth Suteethorn was Thailand's first paleontologist. This sauropod skeleton was the first dinosaur found in Thailand.

DINOSAUR FOOTPRINTS
Footprints must be studied to find out how old they are, what species made them, and what they were doing. Paleontologists put together their story.

Fossilized Clues

Everything we know about dinosaurs has come from the study of fossils. But not even one in every thousand dinosaurs that walked on Earth left bits of fossil evidence behind. That is because conditions have to be just right for an animal to turn into a fossil. Here, a Jurassic *Camptosaurus* has died of disease or old age. If scavengers do not destroy the bones, it will be covered with silt and gradually fossilized.

How Fossils Form

To become a fossil, an animal has to die in the right place, by a river or lake. Then a flood might hit, and its body might get washed into the water, to be buried by mud and sand, and eventually become a fossil. Fossils are found in sandstone, mudstone, limestone, and shale—rocks that started out in rivers, lakes, or the sea.

FROM PLANT TO FOSSIL
If these leaves and pine cones falling into a lake become fossils, every detail except their color will be preserved.

BODY OUT OF REACH

After a dinosaur died, its body was washed into a river. Its flesh rotted or was eaten, and only the skeleton remained.

SKELETON COVER-UP

The skeleton was buried under layers of sand or mud. This protected it from further decay or from being washed away.

BONES INTO FOSSILS

The river sediments turned to rock over time. The bones were replaced by minerals to form fossils, hard like rock.

FOSSILS BACK ON TOP

Movements inside Earth brought the fossil close to Earth's surface. Weather and erosion gradually exposed the fossil.

Discovering Fossils

To find a dinosaur fossil, paleontologists need skill, dedication, and a lot of luck. There are probably countless dinosaur fossils buried all over the world, but the only way to know they are there is if part of a fossil has been exposed by the wind or rain. Dinosaur-rich badlands in Mongolia and North America are the best places to search for dinosaurs.

Hunting for Dinosaurs

A team of paleontologists excavates a Cretaceous bone bed in the Canadian badlands. Some carefully expose the remains of an almost complete duckbill. Others map the skeleton before wrapping the individual bones in plaster and carrying them to their truck. Another group works in the background, excavating a dinosaur skeleton.

CHIPPING AWAY

Mallet

Pick

Most hunting tools can be found in any hardware store.

Detective Work

Dinosaur bone fossils give us clues about what dinosaurs looked like and tell us about how they lived. Individual bones and complete skeletons are the most common dinosaur fossils. From these finds, paleontologists can make theories about dinosaurs and other creatures that lived at the same time.

DILOPHOSAURUS SKELETON
Complete skeletons help us construct the missing pieces of dinosaurs that are known only from fragments, or even single bones.

HADROSAUR BONES
Dinosaur bones tell us what different species were like in life and how they related to each other.

Unusual Fossils

Rarer fossils, such as eggs, dung, and skin impressions, provide valuable clues about how dinosaurs lived. With these extra clues, we can create a more complete picture of dinosaurs and their world.

DINOSAUR EGGS

Possible ornithischian egg

Oviraptor's egg

Fossil finds of eggs and embryos have provided a wealth of information about dinosaur development, reproduction, and behavior.

DUNG FOSSILS

Dinosaur dung that has turned into fossils tells us what dinosaurs ate and how they ate it.

DID YOU KNOW?

The word "fossil" comes from the Latin *fossilis*, and means "dug up."

FEATHER FIBERS

Microraptor fossils from China were covered with feather-like fibers and filaments. Such discoveries provide important details about the link between dinosaurs and birds.

Dinosaur Trackways

Footprints left in rocks show how fast or slowly dinosaurs moved. We know from their tracks that dinosaurs such as long-necks and duckbills travelled in vast herds, while others lived alone. In some cases, we can see dinosaur stories in stone, for example, evidence of a predator scattering a herd or stalking its prey.

STUCK IN THE MUD
Riverbanks were the perfect place for dinosaur footprints to be preserved as fossils.

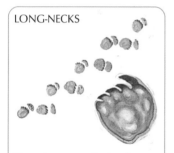

LONG-NECKS

These dinosaurs walked on four feet and left huge back-foot prints.

SMALL MEAT EATERS

Delicate, birdlike tracks show these fast-movers walked on two legs.

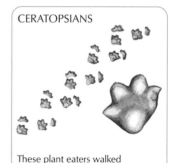

CERATOPSIANS

These plant eaters walked slowly, travelling on four legs.

Preparing Fossils

SAW AND CHISEL

Technicians can spend months patiently freeing a fossil from its casting of rock, called the matrix. They work with hammers, fine chisels, or pneumatic saws.

BLAST AWAY

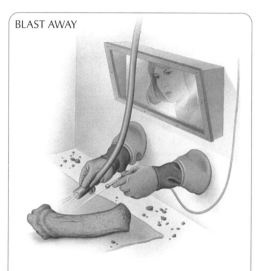

If the fossil bone is harder than sand, technicians use a small shotblaster. Blasts of tiny sand particles erode the rock away. They can also bathe the fossil in acid.

STUCK HARD

The fossil needs to be hardened so it will be preserved forever. Technicians apply special glues and plastics to fossils to make sure they will not fall apart.

FINE FINISH

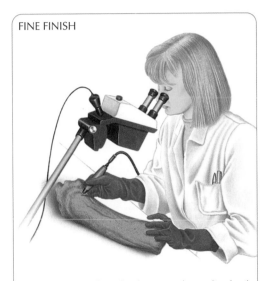

To remove the last bits of rock or to work on a fine fossil, technicians need a microscope. They may use an engraver, a scalpel, a dentist's drill, or even a pin to finish the job.

A DINOSAUR PUZZLE
Each fossil bone is like a puzzle piece. Often,
paleontologists have only a few fragments of
bone. They must study other dinosaur fossils to
work out the shapes of the missing bone pieces.

Dinosaurs on Display

A technician welds metal supports together before this dinosaur fossil goes on display. A strong metal frame is custom built to support and connect each bone. Sometimes, steel wires are attached to the ceiling to hold up long necks or tails or big heads. Dinosaur fossils are very heavy and easily damaged.

Reconstructing a Dinosaur

After carefully studying fossil skeletons to make sure the bones are put together correctly, paleontologists add internal organs—a brain, heart, and so on. We don't really know what dinosaur organs were like because most rotted before they became fossils. Living dinosaur relatives, such as birds and crocodiles, can give good clues. Next, many layers of muscle are added, giving the dinosaur its shape.

AT THE SCENE

These are the only known fossils
of *Baryonyx*. They were found in
a clay pit in southern England.
Scientists are still trying to work out
how this dinosaur is related to others.

The Finishing Touch

Paleontologists know a lot about the texture of dinosaur skin from fossil impressions, but they have to guess what colors the dinosaurs were because colors do not fossilize.

DRAWING DINOSAURS
Dinosaur illustrators work with paleontologists to create an image of what a newly discovered dinosaur looked like. They use color to bring the dinosaur to life.

CHANGING COLOR

Some males may have changed color to mate or to defend territory.

CREATIVE COLOR

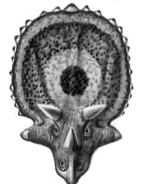  

We do not know what colors dinosaurs were but illustrators can try out ideas.

FINDING OUT MORE

Sites and Museums: USA

The American Museum of Natural History in New York City has the largest collection of dinosaur remains in the world. The Smithsonian Institution's National Museum of Natural History in Washington DC has another large trove. In addition, Utah is home to the Dinosaur National Monument, the most diverse Jurassic dinosaur fossil site in the world.

TYRANNOSAURUS SKELETON
In 1902, an American Museum of Natural History team, led by Barnum Brown, discovered the first *Tyrannosaurus* specimen in Montana.

DINOSAUR BANNER
A large dinosaur banner takes pride of place above the entrance to New York's American Museum of Natural History.

Sites and Museums: Canada

The Dinosaur Provincial Park in Alberta is part of the Canadian badlands. Since the early 1900s, more than 250 dinosaur skeletons and 36 different dinosaur species have been discovered here. The park was named a UNESCO World Heritage Site in 1975, based on its significant dinosaur fossils.

ANCIENT RIVERBEDS
More complete dinosaur skeletons have been found in the Dinosaur Provincial Park, Alberta, than any other dinosaur site on Earth.

THE ROYAL TYRRELL MUSEUM
Found inside the Dinosaur Provincial Park, this is one of the world's most important dinosaur museums.

Sites and Museums: Europe and Britain

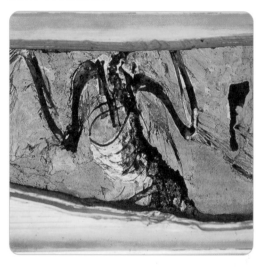

HOLZMADEN AND SOLNHOFEN, GERMANY
These fossil sites in Germany are famous for their finely
preserved fossils such as *Archaeopteryx*, from the Solnhofen
deposits, and marine reptile skeletons at Holzmaden.

LAS HOYAS, SPAIN
The Las Hoyas site, in the mountain ranges of Cuenca
Province, is an ancient lake deposit that has produced some
of the world's best preserved bird and rare dinosaur fossils.

NATURAL HISTORY MUSEUM, LONDON, UK
For the past 200 years, London's Natural History Museum has housed the first dinosaur fossils ever found and described. It has an enormous collection of fossils from around the world.

MUSEUM OF NATURAL HISTORY, PARIS, FRANCE
The Museum of Natural History in Paris houses a wealth of dinosaur fossils from many parts of the world and is a famous center of paleontological research.

Sites and Museums: Mongolia and China

Exciting dinosaur discoveries have been made in the Gobi Desert, Mongolia, since the 1920s. Famous finds here have included the first dinosaur nest and two complete, interlocked dinosaur skeletons. The arms of a *Velociraptor* gripped

FLAMING CLIFFS, XINJIANG
This site in Mongolia has preserved dinosaurs like snapshots in time. Huge sand and dust storms buried them rapidly without warning.

the skull of a *Protoceratops*. Paleontologists think the two dinosaurs were fighting when they were suddenly buried by a freak sandstorm. Recent discoveries in China have shed important new light on the link between birds and dinosaurs.

NEW FOSSILS ON DISPLAY
Teams from the Institute of Vertebrate Paleontology and Paleoanthropology in Beijing search the far corners of China for new fossils like this *Gasosaurus*.

Recent Finds and Sites: Southern Hemisphere

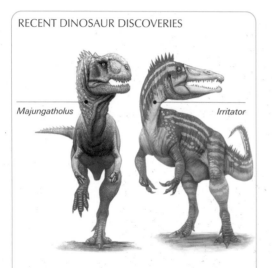

RECENT DINOSAUR DISCOVERIES

Majungatholus

Irritator

In 1993, a perfectly preserved skull of *Majungatholus* was found in Madagascar. *Irritator* was a meat-eating dinosaur recently discovered in Brazil.

South America, southern Africa, and Australia were all part of Gondwana. Searches in these regions have uncovered a range of dinosaurs from all three periods of the Mesozoic era. Recent discoveries are expanding our understanding of the dinosaur world. Paleontologists are learning new things about dinosaurs from each exciting find.

THE VALLEY OF THE MOON, ARGENTINA
The Valley of the Moon is in the province of La Rioja, Argentina. The oldest well-preserved dinosaur fossils, dated to between 226 and 220 million years ago, were found here.

Glossary

badlands The landscape where many dinosaur fossils are found. Badlands are often remote and barren areas where rivers and wind have eroded layers of rock to reveal fossils. There are badlands in Montana, Utah, Wyoming, Colorado, and New Mexico in the USA; in Alberta in Canada; in Patagonia in South America; and in the Gobi desert in China and Mongolia.

Cretaceous period The third and last geological period of the Mesozoic era. It lasted from 144 to 65 million years ago. A great variety of dinosaurs appeared and then became extinct in the Cretaceous.

excavation Uncovering something and then digging it out of the ground.

extinction The dying-out of a species. Dinosaurs became extinct at the end of the Cretaceous period. Their close relatives, the birds, did not.

fossil Any evidence of pre-existing life. It may be the remains of a plant or animal that have turned to stone or have left an impression in rock.

Gondwana The southern supercontinent formed when Pangaea split in two, which began about 208 million years age, during the Jurassic period.

Jurassic period The middle geological period of the Mesozoic era. It lasted from 208 to 144 million years ago. The conditions on Earth were just right for new types of dinosaurs to flourish.

Laurasia The northern supercontinent formed when Pangaea split into two.

matrix The rock still attached to a fossil after it has been dug out of the ground. The matrix is carefully removed from around the fossil by skilled technicians in a laboratory.

meteorite A rocklike object from the remains of a meteoroid that has fallen on Earth.

Mesozoic era The Age of Dinosaurs. It began 245 million years ago, before dinosaurs had evolved, and ended 65 million years ago with a mass extinction of plants and animals. It spanned the Triassic, Jurassic, and Cretaceous periods.

ornithischians The bird-hipped dinosaurs. They had a hip structure where the pubis bone pointed backward, parallel to the ischium. All ornithischians were plant eaters.

pachycephalosaurs The boneheads, a group of plant-eating dinosaurs with skulls thickened into domes of bone. Most lived during the late Cretaceous period in North America and Asia.

paleontologist A scientist who learns about ancient life from studying fossils of plants and animals.

Pangaea The supercontinent that formed in the Permian period and broke up during the Jurassic period.

pterosaurs Flying reptiles appeared during the late Triassic period.

saurischians The lizard-hipped dinosaurs. They had a hip structure where the pubis bone pointed forward. All meat eaters were saurischians. The plant-eating long-necks were also saurischians.

sauropods Long-necked dinosaurs, such as *Diplodocus* and *Brachiosaurus*, with very long necks and tails. They appeared during the late Triassic and included the largest animals to ever walk on Earth.

theropods All the meat-eating dinosaurs. They were lizard-hipped and walked on their back legs.

Triassic period The first geological period in the Mesozoic era, from 248 to 208 million years ago. Dinosaurs appeared about halfway through this period, around 228 million years ago.

Index

Acknowledgements

PHOTOGRAPHS

Key t=top; l=left; r=right; tl=top left; tc=top center; tr=top right; cl=center left; c=center; cr=center right; b=bottom; bl=bottom left; bc=bottom center; br=bottom right

ADL = Ad-Libitum; AMNH = American Museum of Natural History; APL/CBT = Australian Picture Library/Corbis ; ARL = Ardea London; AUS = Auscape International; COR = Corel Corp.; GI = Getty Images; NHM = Natural History Museum, London; PD = Photodisc; PE = PhotoEssentials; QLM = Queensland Museum; WA = Wildlife Art Ltd; WO = Weldon Owen

10bl PE **12**tr PD **15**br ADL **21**t QLM **24**bc, bl, br NHM **26**bl NHM **25**c Peabody Museum of Natural History, Yale University **72**tl ADL/Stuart Bowey **75**cl ADL **103**t GI **105**tc AMNH tr COR **106**bl PD **111**c PD **116**br GI **117**c APL/CBT **118**bl GI **119**c APL/CBT **123**tl APL/CBT tr PE **126**bl, br ADL/Mihal Kaniewski **128**bl AUS **129**c APL/CBT **130**bl, br ADL/Stuart Bowey br NHM **131**bl, br PE r NHM **136**tl NHM **140**bl Oliver Strewe/Wave Productions **144**bl APL/CBT **145**c APL/CBT **146**c APL/CBT **147**bl Royal Tyrrell Museum of Paleontology **148**l Jura Museum, Germany r O. Louis Mazzatenta **149**l NHM r APL/CBT **150**bl WO/George Gerster **151**r Institute of Vertebrate Paleontology and Paleoanthropology, Beijing, China **153**c AUS

ILLUSTRATIONS

Bernard Thornton Artisit UK/Colin Newman, Bernard Thornton Artisit UK/John Francis, Anne Bowman, Andrew Davies/Creative Communication, Simone End, Christer Eriksson, Murray Frederick, Garden Studio/Andrew Robinson, Ray Grinaway, Gino Hasler, James McKinnon, David Kirshner, Frank Knight, Map Illustrations, David McAllister, Stuart McVicar, Paul Newman, Nicola Oram, Peter Bull Art Studio, Peter Schouten, Ray Sim, Marco Sparaciari, Kevin Stead, WA/B. Croucher, WA/Cecilia Fitzsimons, WA/Lee Gibbons, WA/Phil Hood, WA/Mark Iley, WA/Steve Kirk, WA/Luis Rey, WA/Peter Scott, Ann Winterbotham

INDEX

Ken DellaPenta

CONSULTANT

Dr John Long is Head of Sciences at Museum Victoria. His research work as a paleontologist for the past 20 years has focused on fossil fishes and dinosaurs. He is also the author of several popular science books including *Dinosaurs of Australia and New Zealand* (1998) and *Its True! Dinosaurs Never Died* (2004).